Mary Cohen

Beginner repertoire for violin and piano

© 1998 by Faber Music Ltd
First published in 1998 by Faber Music Ltd
3 Queen Square London WC1N 3AU
Cover illustration by Todd O'Neill
Cover design by S & M Tucker
Music processed by Mary Cohen and Jeanne Fisher
Printed in England by Caligraving Ltd

Superpieces 1

with piano accompaniments ISBN 0-571-51869-9
violin part only ISBN 0-571-51871-0

To buy Faber Music publications or to find out about the full range of titles available
please contact your local music retailer or Faber Music sales enquiries:

Faber Music Limited, Burnt Mill, Elizabeth Way, Harlow, CM20 2HX England
Tel: +44 (0)1279 82 89 82
Fax: +44 (0)1279 82 89 83
sales@fabermusic.com
www.fabermusic.com

Openers

(Play along with Famous Tunes)

Melodie

A string

Robert Schumann (1810–1856)
arr. Mary Cohen

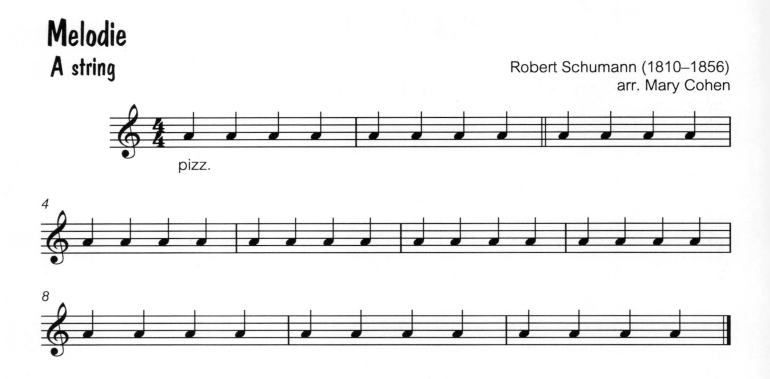

pizz.

Habanera

D string

Georges Bizet (1838–1875)
arr. Mary Cohen

arco

Sailor's Hornpipe
G string

Traditional
arr. Mary Cohen

11 tap screw end of bow gently on music stand

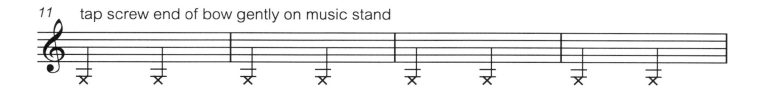

Für Elise
E string

Ludwig van Beethoven (1770–1827)
arr. Mary Cohen

Beasties

Mary Cohen

Active Ants! Active Ants!

wait   wait   wait   wait

Dozing Dino Snores

wait   wait   wait   wait

Galloping Gazelles

wait   *wait*

fading away

Elderly Elephants

Camille Saint-Saëns (1835–1921)
arr. Mary Cohen

el – der – ly   el – e – phants

loud whisper

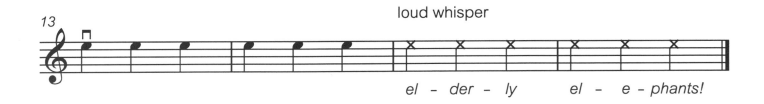

el – der – ly   el – e – phants!

A Day in the Life of an Octopus

Mary Cohen

The Octopus wakes up ...

(one leg at a time)

Listen to the alarm clock

... yawns and stretches ...

(two legs at a time)

... goes downstairs ...

(how many legs at a time?)

... munches breakfast ...

(mmm, fishflakes)

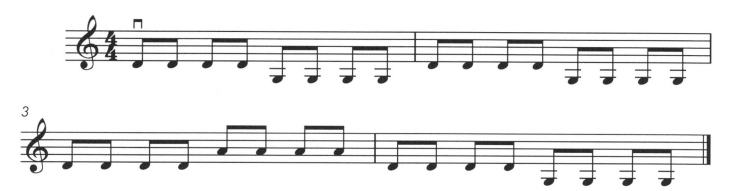

... has a busy time at work ...

(inspecting fish schools)

... comes back home

(and falls asleep in front of the television)

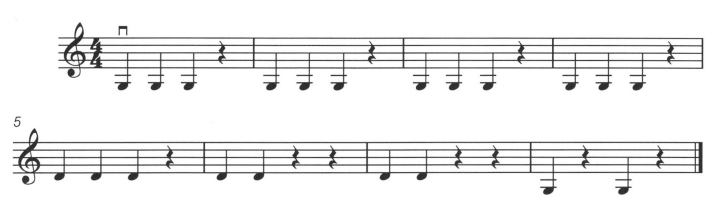

Strange Friends

(lurking in the Witch's House)

Mary Cohen

Batty Bats ...

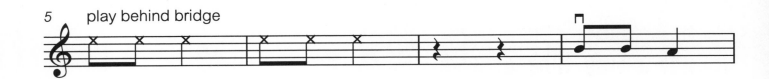

... Ratty Rats ...

... and Black, Black Cats

Disgusting Dinners

(from the Wizard's favourite Cookbook)

Mary Cohen

Slimy Snail Trail Soup

harmonics

Toasted Hedge Trimmings

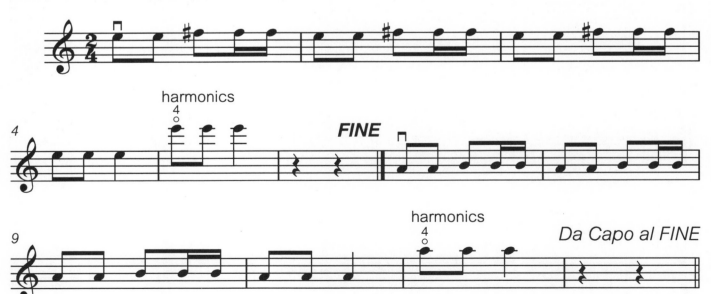

Rotten Eggs with Mouldy Cheese

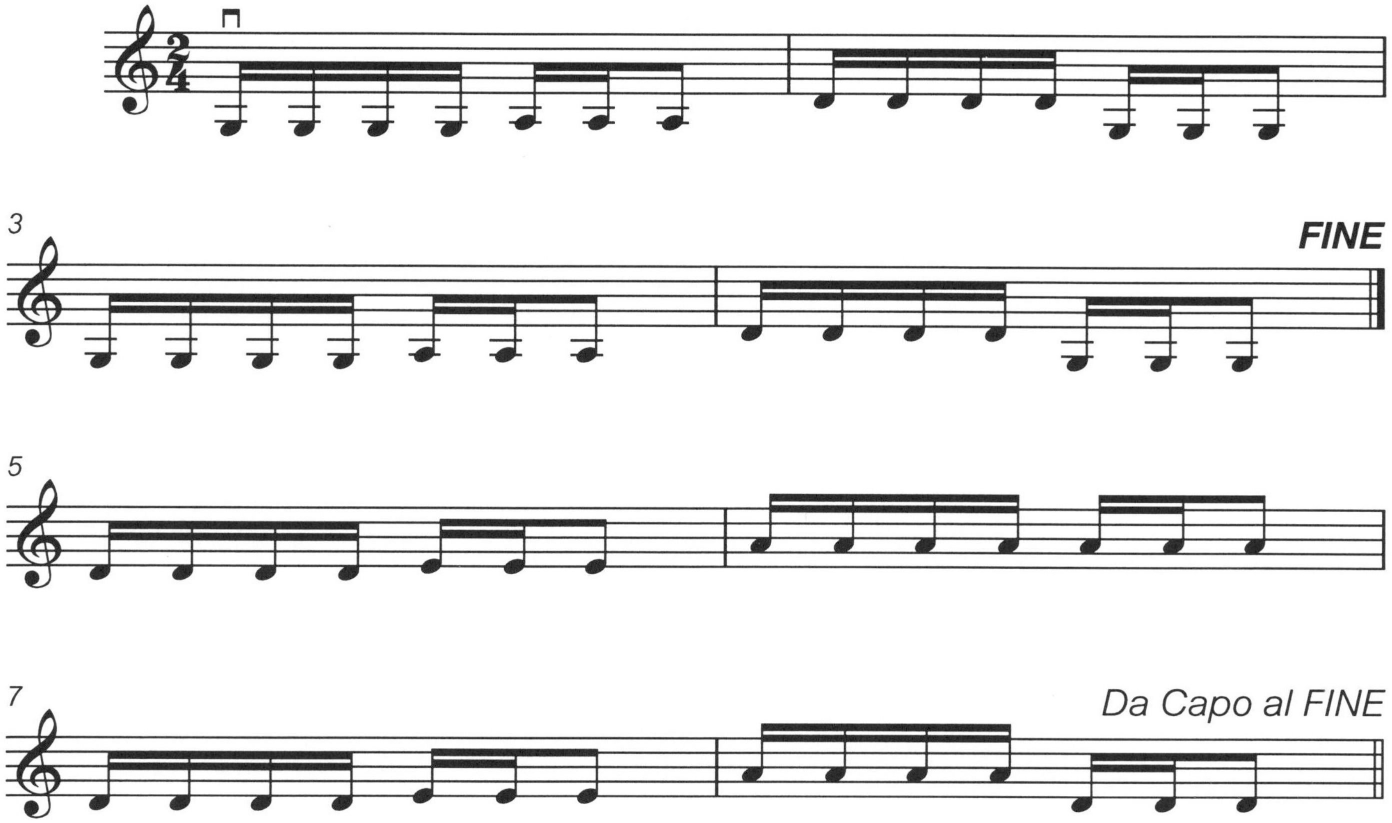

Choc'late Thistle Truffles

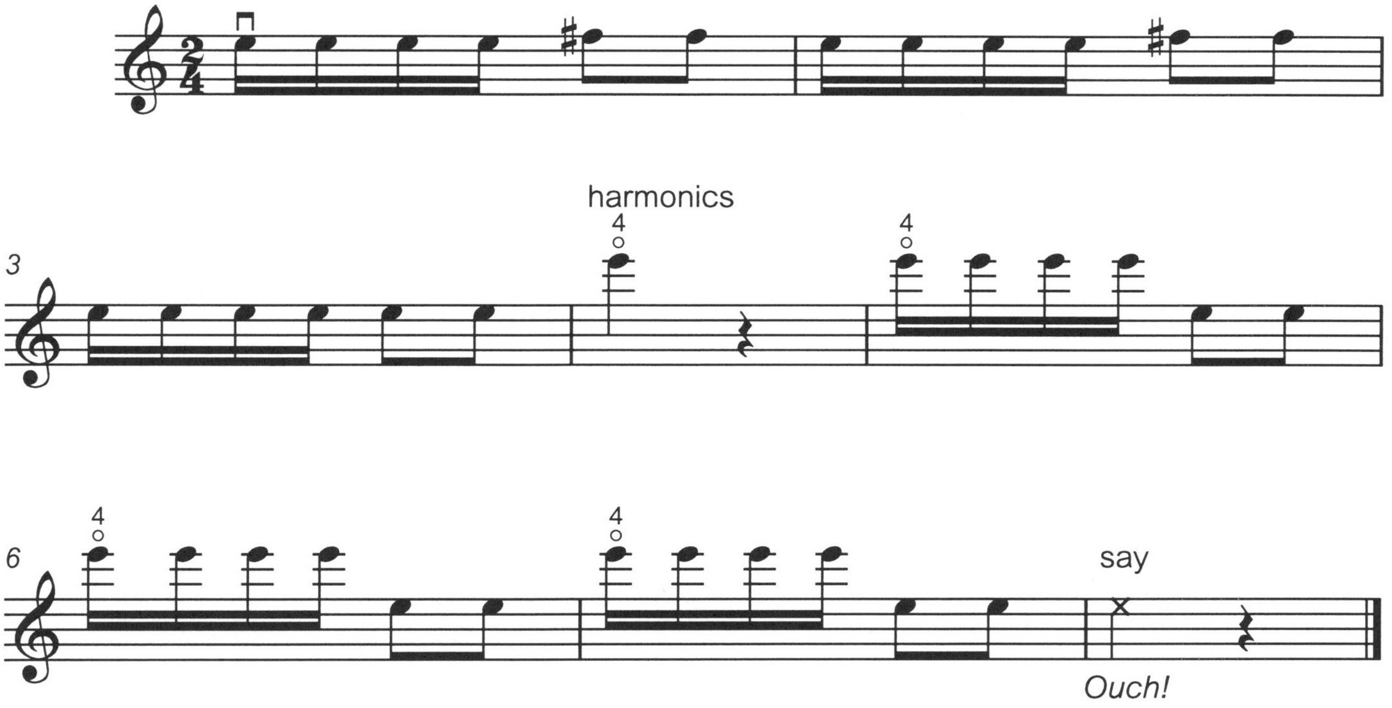

Awkward Moments

Mary Cohen

Feeling awkward ...

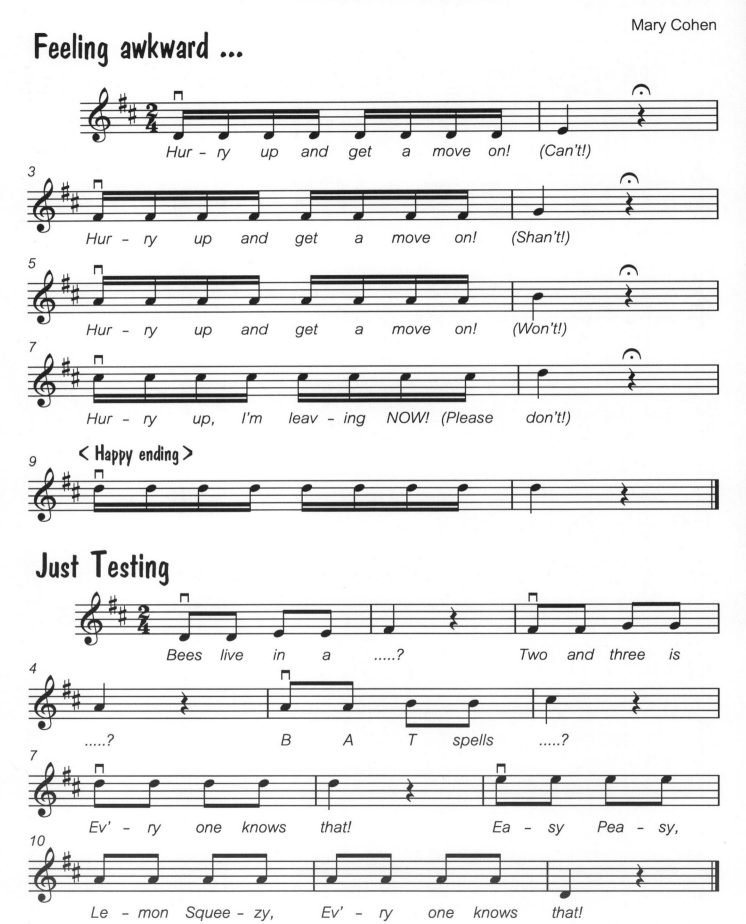

Hur – ry up and get a move on! (Can't!)

Hur – ry up and get a move on! (Shan't!)

Hur – ry up and get a move on! (Won't!)

Hur – ry up, I'm leav – ing NOW! (Please don't!)

< Happy ending >

Just Testing

Bees live in a .....? Two and three is

.....? B A T spells .....?

Ev' – ry one knows that! Ea – sy Pea – sy,

Le – mon Squee – zy, Ev' – ry one knows that!

Oops ...

verse 1

verse 2

(...oops!)

Keep Trying!
(Roadworks and Birthday Bargains)

Mary Cohen

Several years ago ...

'What would you like for your birth - day pre - sent?'

'Pleathe can I have, pleathe can I have,

pleathe can I have a lel - lo did - der?

Juth like the one, juth like the one,

juth like the one out in the woad.'

'No you can't, you're only three!'

A year later ...

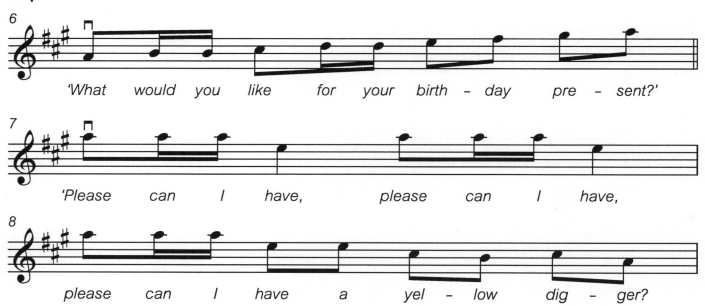

'What would you like for your birth - day pre - sent?'

'Please can I have, please can I have,

please can I have a yel - low dig - ger?

Superpieces 1

Mary Cohen

Beginner repertoire for violin and piano

Piano accompaniments

© 1998 by Faber Music Ltd
First published in 1998 by Faber Music Ltd
3 Queen Square London WC1N 3AU
Cover illustration by Todd O'Neill
Cover design by S & M Tucker
Music processed by Mary Cohen and Jeanne Fisher
Printed in England by Caligraving Ltd

Superpieces 1
with piano accompaniments ISBN 0-571-51869-9
violin part only ISBN 0-571-51871-0

To buy Faber Music publications or to find out about the full range of titles available
please contact your local music retailer or Faber Music sales enquiries:

Faber Music Limited, Burnt Mill, Elizabeth Way, Harlow, CM20 2HX England
Tel: +44 (0)1279 82 89 82
Fax: +44 (0)1279 82 89 83
sales@fabermusic.com
www.fabermusic.com

FABER **ff** MUSIC

Contents

Teacher's Note

Superpieces 1 is a set of pieces for violin with piano accompaniment which can be used either as additional repertoire for pupils working at *Superstart Violin Level 1* or with any mainstream beginner method. All the material uses finger pattern 1 (placing the semitone between the 2nd and 3rd fingers). *Superpieces 1* works equally well in group or individual teaching situations. Skills are introduced gradually and each double-spread contains a suite of pieces which are connected by an overall title. In both fast and slow items the emphasis is on rhythmic fluency, achieved with the help of catchy titles or words. The rhythm in the pupil's part is also frequently supported in the piano accompaniments. Each suite makes a musically satisfying set of concert pieces and the final item is an impressive sounding but simple concertino in three short movements.

Mary Cohen

Superpieces 1			*Superstart Violin Level 1*	
pages	2-3	correlate with	pages	6-11
	4-7			12-15
	8-11			17-26
	12-13			28-29
	14-15			30-40
	16			42-46

Openers

(Play along with Famous Tunes)

Melodie (p. 2)

Robert Schumann (1810–1856)
arr. Mary Cohen

Habanera *(p. 2)*

Georges Bizet (1838–1875)
arr. Mary Cohen

Molto moderato ♩ = 76

Pupil's part written out

Sailor's Hornpipe *(p. 3)*

Traditional
arr. Mary Cohen

Moderato ♩ = 80

Für Elise (p. 3)

Ludwig van Beethoven (1770–1827)
arr. Mary Cohen

Allegretto ♩ = 92

Pupil's part has simplified repeat

Beasties

Mary Cohen

Active Ants! Active Ants! *(p. 4)*

Dozing Dino Snores *(p. 4)*

Galloping Gazelles (p. 5)

Elderly Elephants (p. 5)

Camille Saint-Saëns (1835–1921)
arr. Mary Cohen

loud whisper

el – der – ly el – e – phants!

A Day in the Life of an Octopus

Mary Cohen

The Octopus wakes up ... *(p. 6)*

(one leg at a time)

Andante ♩ = 76

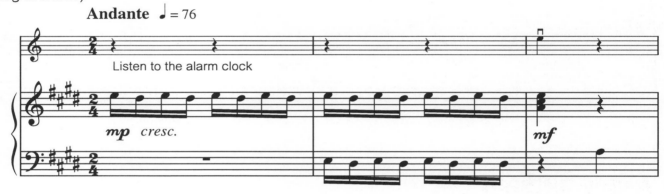

Listen to the alarm clock

mp *cresc.*   *mf*

f

... yawns and stretches ... *(p. 6)*

(two legs at a time)

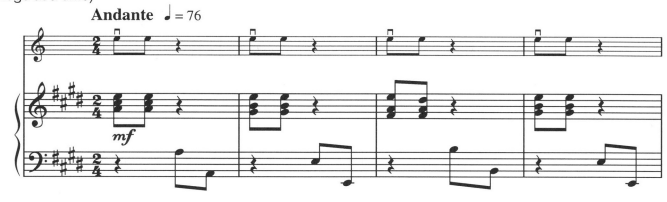

... goes downstairs ... *(p. 6)*

(how many legs at a time?)

... munches breakfast ... (*p. 7*)

(mmm, fishflakes)

... has a busy time at work ... (*p. 7*)

(inspecting fish schools)

optional: LH play quavers

... comes back home *(p. 7)*
(and falls asleep in front of the television)

Strange Friends
(lurking in the Witch's House)

Mary Cohen

Batty Bats ... *(p. 8)*

... Ratty Rats ... (p. 8)

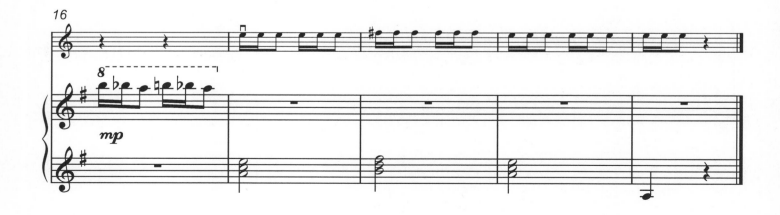

... and Black, Black Cats (p. 9)

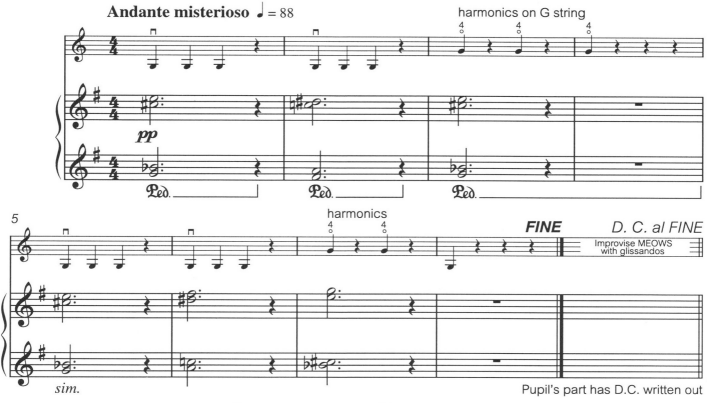

Pupil's part has D.C. written out

Disgusting Dinners

(from the Wizard's favourite Cookbook)

Mary Cohen

Slimy Snail Trail Soup (p. 10)

with pedal

Pupil's part written out

Toasted Hedge Trimmings *(p. 10)*

Rotten Eggs with Mouldy Cheese *(p. 11)*

Choc'late Thistle Truffles *(p. 11)*

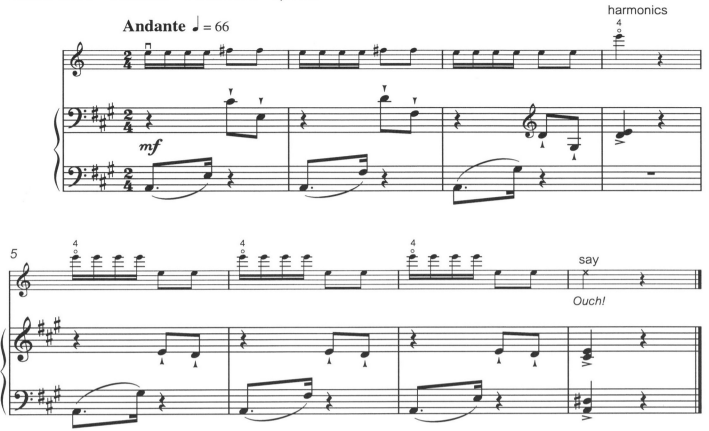

Awkward Moments

Mary Cohen

Feeling Awkward ... *(p. 12)*

Just Testing (p. 12)

Moderato ♩= 66

Oops ... (p. 13)

Allegro moderato ♩= 72

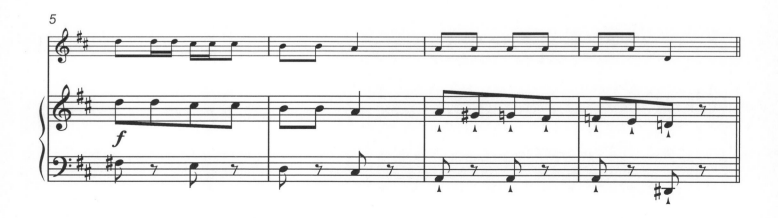

Keep Trying! *(p. 14)*

(Roadworks and Birthday Bargains)

Mary Cohen

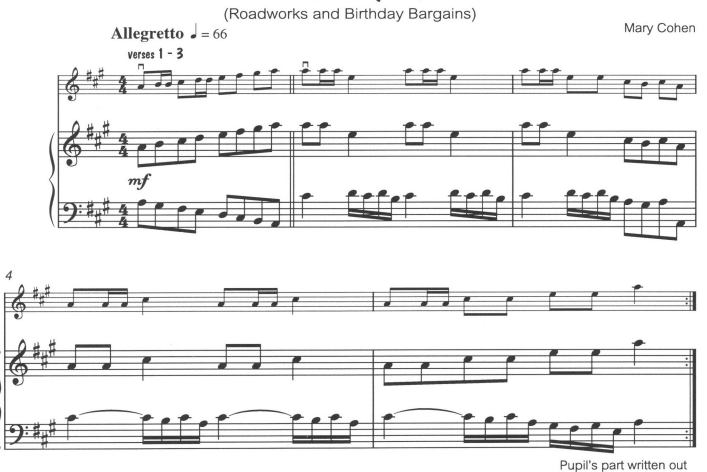

Pupil's part written out

Mini-Concerto

in three movements

Mary Cohen

1. Andantino (*p. 16*)

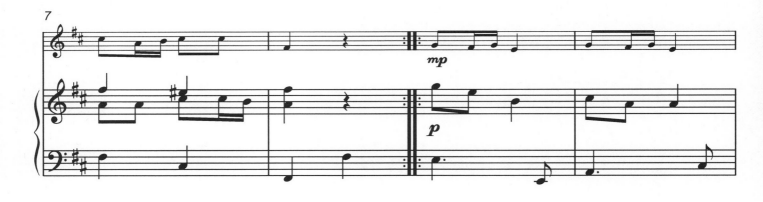

2. Largo (*p. 16*)

3. Allegro moderato (p. 16)

15

Just like the one, just like the one,

just like the one out in the road.'

'No you can't, you're only four!'

The year after that ...

'What would you like for your birth - day pre - sent?'

'Please can I have, please can I have,

please can I have an ex - ca - va - tor?

Just like the one, just like the one,

just like the one out in the road.'

'Of course you can! Just pop upstairs and tidy all your toys away to make room for it.'

(There must be a snag ...)

Mini-Concerto
in three movements

Mary Cohen

1. Andantino

2. Largo

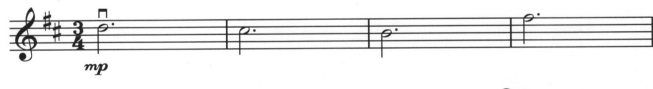

3. Allegro Moderato